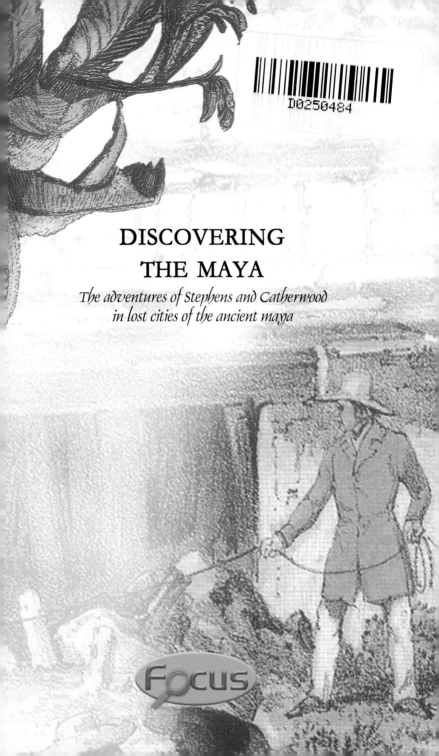

DISCOVERING
THE MAYA

The adventures of Stephens and Catherwood
in lost cities of the ancient maya

Introduction

John L. Stephens was already a well-known travel book author when he decided to explore the lost cities of the Maya. After learning of an exposition in New York by the illustrator Frederick Catherwood, and with his future explorations in mind, Stephens proposed to the artist that they travel to Central America and the Yucatan in search of Maya ruins; Stephens would describe what they found and Catherwood would draw it. Soon thereafter, in 1839, they embarked together on a fabulous adventure through the inhospitable terrain of the ancient Maya world. Upon returning to New York they published their first book, "Incidents of Travel in Central America, Chiapas and Yucatan" (1841). With Stephens's detailed descriptions of the lost cities and Catherwood's stunning illustrations of the Mayan cities of Copán, Quiriguá, Palenque, Uxmal, Chichén Itzá, Tulum and other previously unknown ruins, the book was a best-seller. The following year they returned to Yucatan on a seven-month voyage which culminated in the publishing of their second book, "Incidents of Travel in Yucatan" (1843). Stephens is often referred to as the "Father of Maya Archaeology" because he rescued the cultural riches of this timeless culture. Catherwood's illustrations, however, are what brought the exquisite vision of this culture from the forgotten jungle ruins to the world at large.

Discovering the Maya, part of the Focus series, is an abbreviated version of the travels of Stephens and Catherwood to the lost cities of the ancient Maya. In an effort to revive the vivid emotions of these explorers as they discovered Mayan monuments, we have selected paragraphs from the original text in which Stephens describes their impressions, with illustrations by Catherwood. As a complement to Stephens' descriptions, and to orient the reader in the present, we have included explanatory, up-to-date commentary on each structure, which appears in italics.

Discovering the Maya is a brief, up-to-date look at the adventure of two intrepid travelers and their discovery of the lost cities of the ancient Maya. These cities, buried under the jungle for centuries, had once been the great ceremonial centers of the Maya culture. For Stephens and Catherwood, and now for the present day reader, they stand as impressive testimony to the splendid vision and greatness of this timeless culture.

The Editors

Index

PLATE INDEX

Uxmal

Arrival at the ruins of Uxmal

"In the afternoon, rested and refreshed, we set out for walk to the ruins. The path led through a noble piece of woods, which there were many tracks…[E]merging suddenly from the wood to my astonishment [we] came at once upon a large open field strew with mounds of ruins, and vast buildings on terraces, and pyramic structures, grand and in good preservation, richly ornamented, with out a bush to obstruct the view, and in picturesque effect almost equ to the ruins of Thebes… "

John L. Stephens, Incidents of Travel in Central America, Chiapas and Yuca 1841. Vol. II, pg. 4

Pyramid of the Magiciar

"[…] Drawn off by mounds of ruins and piles of gigan buildings, the eye returns and again fastens upon this lofty structu It was the first building I entered. From its front doorway I count sixteen elevations, with broken walls and mounds of stone, and va magnificent edifices, which at that distance seemed untouched by tir and defying ruin. I stood in the doorway when the sun went dow throwing from the buildings a prodigious breadth of shadow, darke ing the terraces on which they stood, and presenting a scene stran enough for a work of enchantment.

[…] Its form is not pyramidal, but oblong at rounding…and it is protected all around, to the very top, by a wall square stones. […] On the east side of the structure is a broad ran of stone steps…so steep that great care is necessary in ascending at scending…The whole building is of stone; inside, the walls are of polished smoothness; outside, up to the height of the door, the stones are plain and square; and above this line is a rich cornice or moulding, and from this to the top of the building all the sides are covered with rich and elaborate sculptured ornaments, forming a sort of arabesque.

Pyramid of the Magician
The Pyramid of the Magician, called a "House" by Catherwood, is a 32 m (105 ft) high structure that dominates Uxmal. It was built in different stages over many centuries, which explains its architectural diversity and the combination of Chenes and Puuc styles on an oval structure that is quite uncommon in Mayan architecture. It is a massive structure with few openings and appears to have been designed to emphasize visual effects and sacred symbols. External decoration is profuse on the west façade with serpent emblems (a fertility symbol) and masks of Chaac, the rain god. Stephens and Catherwood climbed to the Temple of the Magician on top of the pyramid and admired the serene beauty of the Uxmal, city of sculpted facades.

[…] The designs were strange and incomprehensible, very elaborate, some-mes grotesque, but often simple tasteful and beautiful. Among the intelligible sub-cts are squares and diamonds, with busts of human beings, heads of leopards, and compositions of leaves and flowers, and the ornaments known everywhere as *grecques*. The ornaments, which succeed each other, are all different; the whole form an ex-traordinary mass of richness and complexity, and the effect is both grand and curious…There were no tablets or single stones, each representing by itself an entire object; but every ornament or combination is made up of separate stones, on each of which part of the subject was carved, and which was then set in its place in the wall. Each stone, by itself, was an unmeaning fractional part; but, placed by the side of the others, helped to make a whole, which without it would be incomplete. Perhaps it may, with propriety, be called a species of sculpture mosaic.

The Indians regard these ruins with superstitious reverence. They will not go near them at night, and they have the old story that immense treasure is hidden among them. Each of the buildings has its name given to it by the Indians. This is called the Casa del Anano [sic], or House of the Dwarf, and it is consecrated by a wild legend, which, as I sat in the doorway, I received from the lips of an Indian…"

John L. Stephens, Incidents of Travel in Central America, Chiapas and Yucatan,
1841. Vol. II, pp. 420-423.

Plate of entrance to grand teocalli at Uxmal. Illustration by Frederick Catherwood

Nunnery Quadrangle

"[…] It is called Casa de las Monjas, or House of the Nuns, o the Convent. It is situated on an artificial elevation…[and]…[i]ts form quadrangular…It was not possible to pace all around it, from the masse of fallen stones which encumber it in some places…Like the house the dwarf, it is built entirely of cut stone, and the whole exterior is fille with the same rich, elaborate, and incomprehensible sculptured orna ments.

The principal entrance is by a large doorway into a beautifu patio or courtyard…and the whole inner façade is ornamented mor richly and elaborately than the outside, and in a more perfect state o preservation. On the one side the combination was in the form of di monds, simple, chaste, and tasteful; and at the head of the courtyard tw gigantic serpents, with their heads broken and faller were winding from opposite directions along the who façade."

John L. Stephens, Incidents of Travel in Central Americ Chiapas and Yucatan, 1841. Vol. II, pp. 425-42

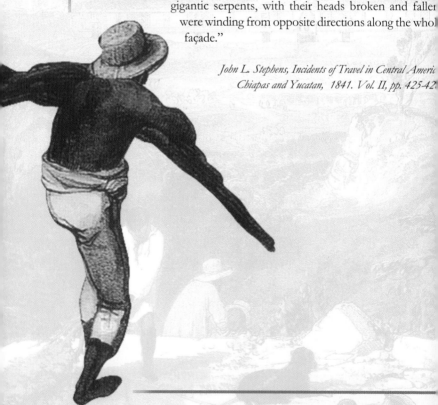

"This building is quadrangular, with a courtyard in the centre. It stands ⌐n the highest of three terraces…

…[A]bove the cornice, from one end to the other, it is ornamented ⌐ith sculpture. In the centre is a gateway…leading to the courtyard. On each ⌐de of the gateway are four doorways with wooden lintels, opening to ⌐oartments…having no communication with each other.

…[A]bove the cornice all are ornamented with the same rich and ⌐aborate sculpture. On the exterior…the designs are simple, and among them ⌐e two rude, naked figures…

Such is the exterior of the building. Passing through the arched gate-⌐ay, we enter a noble courtyard, with four great facades looking down upon it, ⌐ich ornamented from one end to the other with the richest and most intri-⌐ite carving known in the art of the builders of Uxmal; presenting a scene of ⌐range magnificence, surpassing any that is now to be seen in its ruins. […] At ⌐le time of our first visit it was overgrown with bushes and grass, quails started ⌐o from under our feet, and, with a whirring flight, passed over the tops of the ⌐uildings. […]

[…] [T]he side most richly ornamented is so ruined that, under any ⌐rcumstances, it could not be presented entire.

This façade is on the left of the visitor entering the courtyard…It…is ⌐stinguished by two colossal serpents entwined, running through and encom-⌐assing nearly all the ornaments throughout its whole length. […]

[…] The tail of one serpent is held up nearly over the head of the ⌐ther, and has an ornament upon it like a turban, with a plume of feathers. The ⌐arks on the extremity of the tail are probably intended to indicate a rattle-⌐nake, with which species of serpent the country abounds. The lower serpent ⌐as its monstrous jaws wide open, and within them is a human head, the face ⌐f which is distinctly visible on the stone…"

John L. Stephens, Incidents of Travel in Yucatan, 1843. Vol. I, pp. 177-179.

Nunnery Quadrangle

Named for the similarity the conquistadors saw between it and the convent clois-ters of Spain, the Nunnery Quadrangle is considered one of the most outstanding monuments at the ceremonial center of Uxmal. The exquisite decoration and majesty of its structures well deserve the visitors' admiration. It consists of four buildings situated on different levels, all on an immense artificial platform. The facades are covered with carved stone mosaics and masks of the god Chaac, provider of sustenance, representative of water and thus of life itself.

Page 10-11: Plate of general view of nunnery quadrangle at Uxmal.
Ilustration by Frederick Catherwood

House of the Turtles

"[…] It stands at the northwest corner…[and] is called the Casa de las Tortugas, or House of the Turtles, which name was given it by a neighboring cura (priest), from a bead or row of turtles which goes round the cornice…

This building[,]…in size and ornaments[,] contrasts strikingly with the Casa del Gobernador. It wants the rich and gorgeous decoration of the former, but is distinguished for its justness and beauty of proportions, and its chasteness and simplicity of ornament. Throughout there is nothing that borders on the unintelligible or grotesque, nothing that can shock a fastidious architectural taste; but, unhappily, it is fast going to decay.

House of the Turtles. Illustration by Frederick Catherwood.

This building...has [a] peculiar feature, want of convenient access. It has no communication, at least by steps or any visible means, with the Casa del Gobernador, nor were there any steps leading to the terrace below."

John L. Stephens, *Incidents of Travel in Yucatan,*
1843. Vol. I, pp.106-108.

House of the Turtles
The House of the Turtles is noteworthy for the contrast of its comparatively simple, austere facade with its highly decorated frieze. The frieze is highly original and consists of two Puuc-style moldings of uninterrupted, embedded columns. Above the frieze is a border of realistically carved turtles arranged linearly, which give the structure its name.

Page 14-15: Ornament above entrance to grand teocalli at Uxmal.
Illustration by Frederick Catherwood

House of Pigeons

"...[T]he front [of the building] is much ruined, the apartments are filled, and along the centre of the roof, running longitudinally, is a range of structures built in a pyramidal form...These are nine in number, built of stone, ...and have small oblong openings through them. These openings give them somewhat the appearance of pigeon-houses, and from this the name of the building is derived. All had once been covered with figures and ornaments in stucco, portions of which still remain....

In the centre of this building is an archway...which leads into a court-yard... In the centre of the courtyard, and thrown down, is [a] large stone. On the right is a range of ruined buildings, on the left a similar

range, ...rising behind it [a] high mound...; and in front, at the end of the courtyard, is a range of ruined buildings, with another archway in the centre. Crossing the courtyard, and passing through this archway, we ascend a flight of steps, now ruined, and reach another courtyard...On each side of this courtyard, too, is a range of ruined buildings, and at the other end is a great Teocalis... A broad staircase leads to the top, on which stands a narrow building...divided into three apartments.

There was a mournful interest about this great pile of ruins. Entering under the great archway, crossing two noble courtyards, with ruined buildings on each side, and ascending the great staircase to the building on the top, gave a stronger impression of departed greatness than anything else in this desolate city."

John L. Stephens, Incidents of Travel in Yucatan, 1843. Vol. I, pp.193-195.

Pigeon House Quadrangle
Stephens named this nobles residence complex after its high crest perforated by multiple holes, which resembles a pigeon house. The complex consists of four buildings around a rectangular courtyard. The late Puuc-style crest was originally sculpted and painted with reliefs of different people and deities.

House of Pigeons. Ilustration by Frederick Catherwood

Portion of nunnery quadrangle at Uxmal. Illustration by Frederick Catherwood

Governor's Palace

"This was constructed entirely of stone. Up to the cornice which runs round it the whole length and on all four of its sides, the facade presents a smooth surface; above is one solid mass of rich, complicated, and elaborately sculptured ornaments, forming a sort of arabesque.

The grandest ornament, which imparts a richness to the whole facade, is over the centre doorway. Around the head of the principal figure are rows of characters, which, in our first hurried visit, we did not notice as essentially different from the other incomprehensible subjects sculptured on the facade; but we now discovered that these characters were hieroglyphics. […] From their conspicuous position, they no doubt contain some important meaning: probably they were intended as a record of the construction of the building, the time when and the people by whom it was built.

[…] All the other doorways have over them striking, imposing, and even elegant decorations, varying sometimes in the details...

[…] [T]he part immediately over the doorway...shows the remaining portion of a figure seated on a kind of throne. This throne was formerly supported by a rich ornament, still forming part of similar designs over other doorways in this same building. The head-dress is lofty, and from it proceed enormous plumes of feathers, dividing at the top, and all falling symmetrically on each side, until they touch the ornament on which the feet of the statue rest.

[…] This ornament...consists of a stone projecting from the face of the wall...and resembles somewhat an elephant's trunk. […] This projecting stone appears...all over the facade and at the corners; throughout all the buildings it is met with, sometimes in a reversed position...

The rear elevation of the Casa del Gobernador is a solid wall, without any doorways or openings of any kind. Like the front, above the cornice it was ornamented throughout its whole length with sculptured stone. […]"

John L. Stephens, Incidents of Travel in Yucatan,
1843. Vol. I, pp.95-98.

Governor's Palace
The Puuc-style Governor's Palace was built between A.D. 800 and 1000, and consists of a main building with two wings. The facade is smooth, which contrasts with the extremely ornate frieze formed of carved stone mosaics on different planes. It is one of the largest and most important of the structures at Uxmal, and its singular beauty held a fascination for Stephens and Catherwood. Catherwood drew both the ornament above the main entrance and the structure's false arches. His illustration of the ornament shows the exquisite composition of Maya art in its Chaac masks and the figure of a throne where the supreme chief sat, surrounded by plumes (pg. 22). The false arches are one of the most original elements of Mayan architecture, and Catherwood's illustration clearly shows the enormous triangular porticos of this structure (pg. 23), which distinguish it from other buildings at Uxmal.

Page 22: Ornament above main entrance to governor's palace
Page 23: Arched passageway of governor's palace at Uxmal.
Illustration by Frederick Catherwood

Arrival at Kabah

"The next day...we set out for the ruins of Kabah. Our direction was south, on the camino real to Bolonchen...[W]e turned off by a...path..., and [b]eyond we saw through an opening a lofty mound, overgrown, and having on it the ruins of a building...,towering above every other object, and proclaiming the site of another lost and deserted city. Moving on, again, through openings in the trees, we had a glimpse of a great stone edifice, with its front apparently entire. We had hardly expressed our admiration before we saw another, and at a few horses' length a third... We were taken by surprise. Our astonishment and wonder were again roused; and we were almost as much excited as if this was the first ruined city we had seen.

[…]It was absolutely unknown; and the Indians who guided us having conducted us to these buildings, of all the rest seemed as ignorant as ourselves.[…]"

John L. Stephens, Incidents of Travel in Yucatan,
1843. Vol. I, pp.224-226.

Kabah
In Maya, Kabah means "Lord of the strong and powerful hand", which refers to a sculpture at the city entrance depicting a male figure holding a snake in its hand. Kabah was an important city because it was connected with Uxmal and some smaller cities by a 20-km (12.5 mile) long sacbé (white road).

Kabah, Main Teocalli

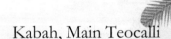

"Following [a] path [from the camino real] towards the field of ruins, the teocalis is the first object that meets [the] eye, grand, picturesque, ruined, and covered with trees...It...rises in a pyramidal form[, and] [a]t the foot is a range of ruined apartments. The steps are fallen, and the sides present a surface of loose stones, difficult to climb, except on one side, where the ascent is rendered practical by the aid of trees. The top presents a grand view. I ascended it for the first time towards evening , when the sun was about setting, and the ruined buildings were casting lengthened shadows over the plain...."

John L. Stephens, Incidents of Travel in Yucatan, 1843. Vol. I, pp.233-235.

Great Pyramid
Known by the nahuatl word "teocalli", the Great Pyramid at Kabah looks much like a natural hill because it was built upon a pre-existing elevation. Its builders took advantage of this elevation to build houses for their gods, which took the form of temples on the pyramid's peak.

Page 26-27: Overview of Kabah. Ilustration by Frederick Catherwood

Kabah, Arch

"...[T]here are on this side of the camino real the remains of other buildings, but all in a ruinous condition, and there is one monument, perhaps more curious and interesting than any that has been presented. It is a lonely arch, of the same form with all the rest...It stands on a ruined mound disconnected from every other structure, in solitary grandeur. Darkness rests upon its history, but in that desolation and solitude, among the ruins around, it stood like the proud memorial to a Roman triumph. Perhaps, like the Arch of Titus, which at this day spans the Sacred Way at Rome, it was erected to commemorate a victory over enemies.

John L. Stephens, Incidents of Travel in Yucatan,
1843. Vol. I, pp.246-247.

Arch at Kabah
The Arch was built in the ancient Puuc style and is the only restored monument in this section of the site. It served to mark the beginning of the sacbé connecting Kabah to Uxmal. The decoration was sober and it was painted a red color, portions of which are still visible. Stephens and Catherwood beautifully documented the Arch (pg. 30) during their visit.

Kabah, Structure I

"...[T]he moment we saw [this building] we were struck with the extraordinary richness and ornament of its facade...

The ornaments are of the same character with those at Uxmal, alike complicated and incomprehensible, and from the fact that every part of the facade was ornamented with sculpture, even the portion now buried under the lower cornice, the whole must have presented a greater appearance of richness than any building at Uxmal. The cornice running over the doorways, tried by the severest rules of art recognised among us, would embellish the architecture of any known era...

The lintels of the doorways were of wood; these are all fallen, and of all the ornaments which decorated them not one now remains. No doubt they corresponded in beauty of sculpture with the rest of the facade. The whole now lies a mass of rubbish and ruin at the foot of the wall.

On the top is a structure which, at a distance, as seen indistinctly through the trees, had an appearance of a second story, and, as we approached, it reminded us of the towering structures on the top of some of the ruined buildings at Palenque."

John L. Stephens, Incidents of Travel in Yucatan,
1843. Vol. I, pp.235-237.

Kodz Poop
In Maya, Kodz Poop means "rolled mat". It is a master work of decorative sculpture with a facade richly adorned with Chaac masks, which were thought to be elephants by early visitors. Catherwood made an extraordinary illustration of the building's interior (pg 31) showing its two parallel rooms connected by two steps coming out of the hooked nose of a carved Chaac mask.

Page 30: Arch at Kabah.
Page 31:Interior of main structure at Kabah.
Illustration by Frederick Catherwood

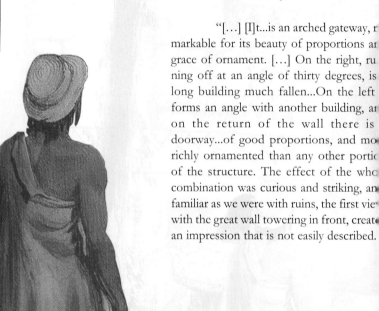

Labna

Labna, Arch

"[…] [I]t...is an arched gateway, re
markable for its beauty of proportions and
grace of ornament. […] On the right, run
ning off at an angle of thirty degrees, is a
long building much fallen...On the left it
forms an angle with another building, and
on the return of the wall there is a
doorway...of good proportions, and more
richly ornamented than any other portion
of the structure. The effect of the whole
combination was curious and striking, and
familiar as we were with ruins, the first view
with the great wall towering in front, created
an impression that is not easily described."

[…] [P]assing through (the gateway) ...we entered a thick forest, growing so close upon the building that we were unable to make out even its shape; but, on clearing away the trees, we discovered that this had been the principal front, and that these trees were growing in what had once been the area, or courtyard. The doors of the apartments on both sides of the gateway...opened upon this area. Over each doorway was a square recess, in which were the remains of a rich ornament in stucco, with marks of paint still visible, apparently intended to represent the face of the sun surrounded by its rays, probably once objects of adoration and worship, but now willfully destroyed."

John L. Stephens, Incidents of Travel in Yucatan,
1843. Vol. II, pg. 34.

Arch at Labna
Because of its distinctive decoration and design, the Arch at Labna is considered one of the architectural masterpieces of the ancient Maya of Yucatan. It consists of an arched passage with two lateral portions, each with a door decorated with geometric elements simulating serpents. Stephens described the frieze in detail, but it was not until later that it was seen to be a stylized Mayan house, and what he had thought to be objects of worship and adoration were actually richly adorned Mayan nobles sitting inside the houses. The arch originally had a crest, of which only a remnant remains, but its east facade is still richly ornamented with columns and lattices, and the corners still have Chaac masks.

Page 34-35: Arch at Labna. Ilustration by Frederick Catherwood

Bolonchen

Bolonchen Caves

"We disencumbered ourselves of superfluous appare and, following the Indian, each with a torch in hand, entered wild cavern, which, as we advanced, became darker. At the di tance of sixty paces the descent was precipitous, and we we down by a ladder about twenty feet. Here all light from the mou of the cavern was lost, but we soon reached the brink of a gre perpendicular descent, to the very bottom of which a strong bo of light was thrown from a hole in the surface...As we stood c the brink of this precipice, under the shelving of an immens mass of rock, seeming darker from the stream of light throw down the hole, gigantic stalactites and huge blocks of stone a sumed all manner of fantastic shapes, and seemed like monstrou animals or deities of a subterranean world.

From the brink on which we stood an enormous lad der, of the rudest possible construction, led to the bottom the hole. It was...made of the rough trunks of saplings lashe together lengthwise and supported all the way down by horizor tal trunks braced against the face of the precipitous rock. Th ladder was double, having two sets or flights of rounds, divide by a middle partition, and the whole fabric was lashed togeth by withes. It was very steep, seemed precarious and insecure, ar confirmed the worst accounts we had heard of the descent in this remarkable well.

Our Indians began the descent, but the foremost ha scarcely got his head below the surface before one of the round slipped, and he only saved himself by clinging to another. [.. We attempted a descent with some little misgivings, but, by keep ing each hand and foot on a different round, with an occasion crash and slide, we all reached the foot of the ladder...

..] Looking up, the view of its broken sides, with the light thrown own from the orifice above, was the wildest that can be conceived. As yet the reader is only at the mouth of this well; but, to xplain to him briefly it extraordinary character, I give it its name, hich is Xtacumbi Xunan. The Indians understand by this La eñora escondida, or the lady hidden away; and it is derived from fanciful Indian story that a lady stolen from her mother was oncealed by her lover in this cave".

John L. Stephens, Incidents of Travel in Yucatan,
1843. Vol. II, pp. 98-100.

Bolonchen Cave
The word Bolonchen is composed of two Mayan words, "bolon", which means nine, and "chen" which means well. This refers to the nine wells that have formed the center of the town for centuries and which are still located in the main plaza. Located in a region of limestone perforated with natural caves, Bolonchen was an important water source for the ancient Maya. The Bolonchen caves are extremely deep, but given the scarcity of surface water in the area, the Maya figured out how to descend into them to extract this liquid treasure. In addition to the precious water, the caves also hold the remains and mysteries of their ancient users. Catherwood's illustration shows the double wood pole ladder that descended into the caves, as seen from the bottom.

Page 38-39: Well at Bolonchen. Ilustration by Frederick Catherwood

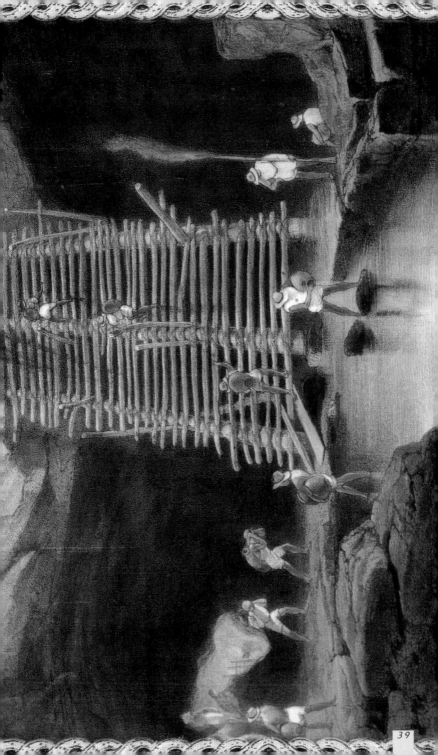

Chichen Itza

The Nunnery

"[…] [I]t is remarkable for its good state of preservation, and th
richness and beauty of its ornaments...It has two cornices of tasteful an
elaborate design. Over the doorway are twenty small cartouches of hiero
glyphics in four rows, five in a row...Over these stand out in a line six bol
projecting curved ornaments, like that presented from the House of th
Governor at Uxmal, resembling an elephant's trunk, and the upper centr
space over the doorway is an irregular circular niche, in which portions of
seated figure, with a headdress of feathers, still remain. The rest of the orna
ments are of that distinctive stamp, characteristic of the ancient America
cities, and unlike the designs of any other people...
[…] [T]he front of the same building...is composed of two structures entirel
different from each other. […] The only portion containing interior cham
bers is that which I have called the wing. This has two doorways opening int
chambers...behind each of which is another of correspondin
dimensions...The whole number of chambers in this wing is nine, and thes
are all apartments on the ground floor. […] A grand staircase..., the largest w
saw in the country, rises to the top. On one side of the staircase a hug
breach...has been made by the proprietor, for the purpose of getting ou
building stone...

John L. Stephens, Incidents of Travel in Yucata
1843. Vol. II, pg. 19

The Nunnery at Chichen Itza

The Nunnery is one of the most distinctive architectural groups at Chichen Itza. Especia
notable is the structure on the east side of the group (pp 42-43), which is a masterpiece of P
art. Its facade is complex but maintains a balance despite the profusion of elements within it. .
the time of Stephens and Catherwood's visit these elements were thought to be purely decorat
but Catherwood understood that they held meaning and he called them hieroglyphics. Today th
are known as glyphs and they form part of Mayan writing, which has only recently been decoa

"[...] It has three cornices, and the spaces between are richly ornamented. the sculpture is rude but grand. The principal ornament is over the
doorway, and on each side are two human figures in a sitting posture, but,
unfortunately, much mutilated. The portion of the facade above the second
cornice is merely an ornamented wall, like those before mentioned at Zayi
and Labna.

The whole of this building is in a good state of preservation. The
interior consists of a single apartment, once covered with plaster, and along
the top of the wall under the arch are seen the traces of a line of medallions
or cartouches in plaster, which once contained hieroglyphics. The Indians
have no superstitious feelings about these ruins, except in regard to this building; and in this they say that on Good Friday of every year music is heard
sounding; but this illusion...was here destined to be broken. In this chamber
we opened our Daguerreotype apparatus, and on Good Friday were
at work all day, but heard no music...

John L. Stephens, Incidents of Travel in Yucatan,
1843. Vol. II, pg. 198.

<u>The Church</u>
Stephens and Catherwood spent the calm-
est days of their voyage at Chichen Itza,
enjoying their host's hospitality and recov-
ering from malaria. While there
Catherwood measured the ruins, copied the
bas-reliefs and drew the beautiful monu-
ments, including the Church. This struc-
ture forms part of the Nunnery group. Its
facade is composed of two large ornamented
friezes between three cornices, each of which
terminates in a Chaac mask at the corners.
Above the first frieze is a molding in the
form of a serpent followed by another
molding of stepped Greek designs and
finally the second frieze containing three
large Chaac masks.

The Church. Ilustration by Frederick Catherwood

The nunnery at Chichen Itza. Illustration by Frederick Catherwood

The Castillo

"[…] [T]he Castillo…[is] the first building we saw, a[nd] from every point of view the grandest and most conspicuo[us] object that towers above the plain. Every Sunday the ruins a[re] resorted to as a promenade by the villagers of Piste, and nothi[ng] can surpass the picturesque appearance of this lofty buildi[ng] while women, dressed in white, with red shawls, are movi[ng] on the platform, and passing in and out of the doors. […] [It] does not face the cardinal points exactly, though probably [so] intended; and all the buildings, from some cause not eas[ily] accounted for, while one varies ten degrees one way, th[at] immediately adjoining varies twelve to thirteen degrees [in] another. It is built apparently solid from the plain…On t[he] west side is a staircase…on the north…the staircase contai[ns] ninety steps. On the ground at the front of the staircas[e] forming a bold, striking and well-conceived commenceme[nt] to this lofty range, are two colossal serpents' heads…wi[th] mouths wide open and tongues protruding…No doubt th[ey] were emblematic of some religious belief, and in the minds [of] an imaginative people, passing between them to ascend t[he] steps, must have excited feelings of solemn awe.

The platform at the top of the mound…[has] [s]ing[le] doorways [that] face the east, south, and west, having massi[ve] lintels of sapote wood covered with elaborate carvings, a[nd] the jambs are ornamented with sculpted figures…The scul[p] ture is much worn, but the head-dress, ornamented with [a] plume of feathers, and portions of the rich attire still remai[n]. The face is well preserved and has a dignified appearance. [It] has, too, earrings and the nose bored, which, according to t[he] historical accounts, was so prevalent a custom in Yucatan, th[at] long after the conquest the Spaniards passed laws for its pro[] hibition.

All the other jambs are decorated with sculpture of the same neral character, and all open into a corridor...extending round three les of the building.

The doorway facing the north...presents a grander pearance...having two short massive columns...with two large pro- ctions at the base, entirely covered with elaborate sculpture. This orway gives access to a corridor...In the back wall of this corridor is ingle doorway, having sculptured jambs, over which is a richly-carved pote beam…giving entrance to an apartment...The impression pro- ced on entering this lofty chamber, so entirely different from all we d met with before, was perhaps stronger than any we had yet expe- nced. We passed a whole day within it, from time to time stepping t upon the platform to look down upon the ruined buildings of the cient city, and an immense field stretching on all sides beyond".

John L. Stephens, Incidents of Travel in Yucatan,
1843. Vol. II, pp. 213-217.

<u>*The Castillo or Pyramid of Kukulkan*</u>
While visiting Chichen Itza, Stephens and Catherwood noted that many of the buildings were not oriented according to the cardinal points. At this time the sophistication of Mayan astronomical knowledge was still unknown, and it was not until many years later that it was discovered that the pyramids and palaces at Chichen Itza were oriented according to stars, constellations and planets such as Mercury, Venus, Mars, Jupiter, and probably Saturn. The Castillo, or Teocalli, is a pyramid with nine steps, measuring 60 m (197 ft) on each side by 24 m (79 ft) tall, and is located in the center of the site's main plaza. A staircase ascends each side of the pyramid to a temple decorated with serpents and jaguars, where the famous chacmool sculpture was found. The pyramid visible today was built in the 13th Century AD, but inside this later pyramid is a smaller pyramid built two centuries earlier. Inside this second pyramid is a jaguar throne with jade inlays.

Page 46-47: Teocalli at Chichen Itza. Ilustration by Frederick Catherwood

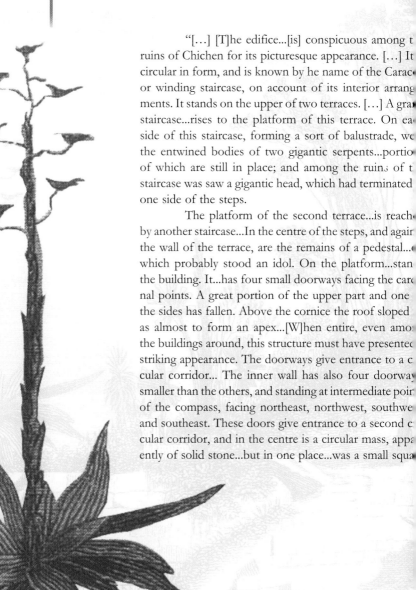

The Observatory

"[…] [T]he edifice…[is] conspicuous among t
ruins of Chichen for its picturesque appearance. […] It
circular in form, and is known by he name of the Carac
or winding staircase, on account of its interior arrang
ments. It stands on the upper of two terraces. […] A gra
staircase…rises to the platform of this terrace. On ea
side of this staircase, forming a sort of balustrade, we
the entwined bodies of two gigantic serpents…portio
of which are still in place; and among the ruins of t
staircase was saw a gigantic head, which had terminated
one side of the steps.

The platform of the second terrace…is reach
by another staircase…In the centre of the steps, and agair
the wall of the terrace, are the remains of a pedestal…
which probably stood an idol. On the platform…stan
the building. It…has four small doorways facing the car
nal points. A great portion of the upper part and one
the sides has fallen. Above the cornice the roof sloped
as almost to form an apex…[W]hen entire, even amo
the buildings around, this structure must have presente
striking appearance. The doorways give entrance to a c
cular corridor… The inner wall has also four doorway
smaller than the others, and standing at intermediate poir
of the compass, facing northeast, northwest, southwe
and southeast. These doors give entrance to a second c
cular corridor, and in the centre is a circular mass, appa
ently of solid stone…but in one place…was a small squa

pening choked up with stones, which I endeavored to clear
ut; but the stones falling into the narrow corridor made it
angerous to continue. The roof was so tottering that I could
ot discover to what this opening led. It was about large
nough to admit the figure of a man in a standing position, to
ok out from the top. The walls of both corridors were plas-
red and ornamented with paintings, and both were covered
ith the triangular arch. The plan of the building was new,
ut instead of unfolding secrets, it drew closer the curtain
at already shrouded, with almost impenetrable folds, these
ysterious structures".

John L. Stephens, Incidents of Travel in Yucatan,
1843. Vol. II, pp. 198-200.

The Caracol or Observatory

*Stephens and Catherwood deduced that significant
changes had occurred in the city because they noticed
that only certain structures at Chichen Itza were built
in the Puuc style. Others such as the Castillo, the Ball
Court and the Temple of Warriors, were built in a
distinctive, later style known as Maya-Toltec. The
Caracol is also from this period and was built as an
astronomical observatory to track the movements of the
planet Venus. Built atop two platforms, the main structure is circular and has an interior spiral staircase that
leads to a room with square openings in the walls. These
openings apparently functioned as astronomical obser-
vation windows.*

Page 50-51: The caracol at Chichen Itza.
Illustration by Frederick Catherwood

The Ball Court

"It consists of two immense parallel walls...or hundred and twenty feet apart...[F]acing the open spac between the walls stands on an elevation building...containing a single chamber, with the from fallen, and, rising among the rubbish, the remains two columns, elaborately ornamented with sculptur the whole interior wall being exposed to view, covere from the floor to the peak of the arch with sculpture figures in bas-relief, much worn and faded. [...] [A the other end, setting back, is another building...als ruined, but exhibiting the remains of two columns rich ornamented with sculpted figures in bas-relief. [...]

In the centre of the great stone walls, exact opposite each other...are two massive stone rings...C the rim and border were two sculpted entwined se pents...

These walls, at the first glance, we considere identical in their uses and purposes with the parall structures supporting the rings at Uxmal, of which have already expressed the opinion that they were ir tended for the celebration of some public games".

John L. Stephens, Incidents of Travel in Yucata
1843. Vol. II, pg. 20

Page 54-55: Ball court at Chichen Itza.
Ilustration by Frederick Catherwo

Ball Court

The two travelers were quite interested in the Ball Court. Catherwood drew one of the stone rings richly decorated with the Plumed Serpent, and Stephens, who correctly deduced the use of the court for a game, found a deteriorated mural in the Temple of Jaguars that he thought depicted a naval battle. The Ball Court at Chichen Itza is the largest in Mesoamerica and has an architecture that is clearly Toltec-influenced. The main area, or playing field, is flanked by two enormous walls, each with a stone ring decorated with a serpent situated at what would be center field. The lower portion of the walls are decorated with bas-reliefs recording the meeting of two teams and the decapitation of one of the team captains.

Tulum

The Castillo

"In the afternoon we set out for the ruins of Tuloom, a leagu[e] distant on the coast, and with the Castillo on a high cliff in full sight.

[...] [W]e entered a gloomy forest, and, passing a building o[n] the left, with 'old walls' visible in different places indistinctly through th[e] trees, reached the grand staircase of the Castillo. The steps, the platform of the building, and the whole area in front were overgrown with tree[s] large and principally ramon, which, with their deep green foliage and th[e] mysterious buildings around, presented an image of a grove sacred t[o] Druidical worship.

[...] [I]mpediments and difficulties had accumulated upon u[s] but already we felt indemnified for our labour. We were amid the wilde[st] scenery we had yet found in Yucatan; and, besides the deep and excitin[g] interest of the ruins themselves, we had around us what we wanted at a[ll] other places, the magnificence of nature. Clearing away the platform i[n] front, we looked over an immense forest.; walking around the mouldin[g] of the wall, we looked upon the boundless ocean, and deep in the clea[r] water at the foot of the cliff we saw gliding quietly by a great fish.

[...] The grand staircase...with twenty-four steps, and a substan[-] tial balustrade on each side, still in good preservation, gives it an unusu[-] ally imposing character. In the doorway are two columns, making thre[e] entrances, with square recesses above them, all of which contained orna[-] ments, and in the centre one fragments of a statue still remain.
The interior is divided into two corridors...the one in front [having] [at] each end a stone bench, or divan; again on the walls we found the myste[-] rious print of the red hand.

A single doorway leads to the back corridor...[which] has a stone bench [ex]tending along the foot of the wall. On each side of the doorway are stone [ri]ngs, intended for the support of the door, in the back wall are oblong open[in]gs, which admit breezes from the sea. Both apartments have the triangular-[ar]ched ceiling...

The wings are much lower than the principal building. Each consists [of] two ranges, the lower standing on a low platform, from which are steps [le]ading to the upper. The latter consists of two chambers, of which the one in [fr]ont...[has] two columns in the doorway, and two in the middle of the chamber [co]rresponding with those in the doorway. The centre columns were ornamented [wi]th devices in stucco, one of which seemed a masked face, and the other the [he]ad of a rabbit. [...] From this apartment a doorway...close to the wall of the [pr]incipal building, leads to a chamber..also roofless, and having the same indica-[ti]ons that the roof had been flat and supported by wooden beams.

[...] [T]he back or sea wall of the Castillo...rises on the brink of a high, [br]oken, precipitous cliff, commanding a magnificent ocean view, and a pictur-[es]que line of coast, being itself visible from a great distance at sea. The wall is [so]lid, and has no doorways or entrances of any kind, nor even a platform around [...]

John L. Stephens, Incidents of Travel in Yucatan,
1843. Vol. II, pp. 262-266.

The Castillo at Tulum

Stephens and Catherwood called Mayan rooms "corridors" because they are much narrower than European-style rooms. This is because the Maya, or "false", arch used in Maya structures cannot cover wide spaces, which limits rooms to long, narrow spaces. Tulum was a Maya city built on the edge of sea cliffs overlooking the Caribbean Sea. It reached its peak between A.D. 900 and 1200, when it was the largest port on the Mayan coastal trading routes which ran as far as current day Honduras. The Castillo was a sacred place used for religious ceremonies. It is the highest building at Tulum and for this reason was the first Mayan construction seen by the Spanish when they arrived at the coasts of Yucatan in 1518.

The castillo at Tulum. Illustration by Frederick Catherwood

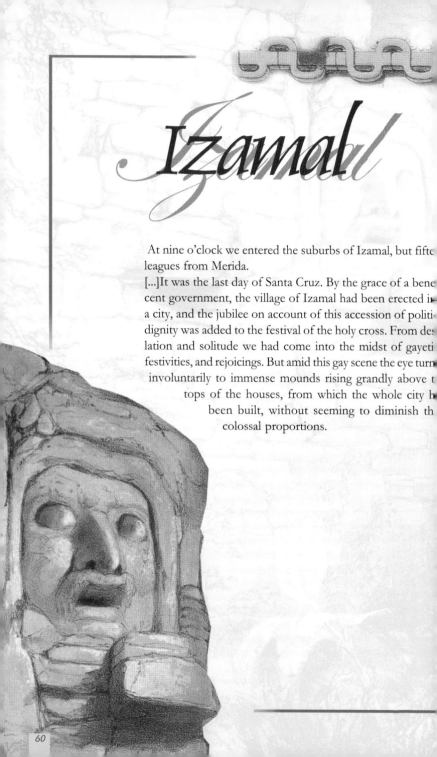

Izamal

At nine o'clock we entered the suburbs of Izamal, but fifte
leagues from Merida.

[...]It was the last day of Santa Cruz. By the grace of a bene
cent government, the village of Izamal had been erected i
a city, and the jubilee on account of this accession of politi
dignity was added to the festival of the holy cross. From des
lation and solitude we had come into the midst of gayeti
festivities, and rejoicings. But amid this gay scene the eye turn
involuntarily to immense mounds rising grandly above t
tops of the houses, from which the whole city h
been built, without seeming to diminish th
colossal proportions.

ne of these great mounds, having at that time benches upon
commanding a view of the bull – fight in the plaza, blocked
the yard of the house we occupied, and extended into the
joining yard of the Señora Mendez, who was the owner of
oth. It is, perhaps, two hundred feet long and thirty high. The
rt in our yard was entirely ruined, but in that of the señora it
ppeared that its vast sides had been covered from one end to
e other with colossal ornaments in stucco, most of which
d fallen, but among the fragments is the gigantic. It is seven
et eight inches in height and seven feet in width. The ground-
ork is of projecting stones, which are covered with tucco. A
one one foot six inches long protrudes from the chin, in-
ded, perhaps, for burning copal on, as a sort of altar.

John L. Stephens, Incidents of Travel in Yucatan,
1843. Vol. II, pp. 282-292.

Izamal

*Izamal was likely one of the most important of the Mayan
cities of Yucatan. It was a city of many pyramids, but has
the distinction of being the site of the largest pyramid in
Yucatan. A colossal head sculptured out of stucco that rep-
resented a god and was used to burn copal once adorned the
side of one of Izamal's pyramids. This head was later destroyed as the city grew. Catherwood drew the head during
his visit, providing an invaluable record of this lost treasure,
which highlights the enormous documentary value of
Catherwood's work.*

Page 62-63: Colossal head at Izamal. Ilustration by Frederick Catherwood

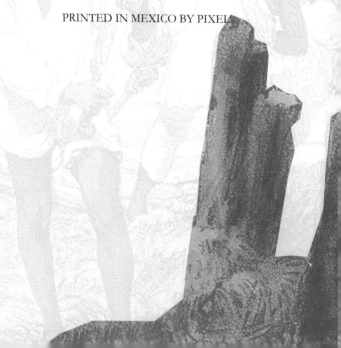

DISCOVERING THE MAYA
The adventure of Stephens and Catherwood
in lost cities of the ancient maya
2nd Edition, 2006

All Rights Reserved © Editorial Dante S.A de C.V.
Calle 19 No. 102 x 20 Col. México. C.P. 97125
Mérida, Yucatán, México.

I.S.B.N. 970-605-257-7

Producer in chief: Hervé Baeza Braga
Project Director: Javier Covo Torres
Frontispiece and Inner Design: Anilú Morales Valencia
Text: Dante archives

PRINTED IN MEXICO BY PIXEL